The Horse
and the
Plains Indians

The Horse
and the
Plains Indians

A POWERFUL PARTNERSHIP

DOROTHY HINSHAW PATENT

Photographs by WILLIAM MUÑOZ

Clarion Books | Houghton Mifflin Harcourt | Boston   New York | 2012

CLARION BOOKS

215 Park Avenue South, New York, New York 10003

Text copyright © 2012 by Dorothy Hinshaw Patent

Photographs copyright © 2012 by William Muñoz, except where otherwise credited

Clarion Books is an imprint of Houghton Mifflin Harcourt Publishing Company.

www.hmhbooks.com

The text of this book was set in Spectrum MT.

Library of Congress Cataloging-in-Publication Data

Patent, Dorothy Hinshaw.

The horse and the Plains indians : a powerful partnership / written by Dorothy Hinshaw Patent ;

photos by William Muñoz.

p. cm.

ISBN 978-0-547-12551-0

1. Indians of North America—Domestic animals—Great Plains—Juvenile literature. 2. Horses—Great Plains—

History—Juvenile literature. 3. Human-animal relationships—Great Plains—History—Juvenile literature. I. Title.

E78.G73P357 2012

978.004'97352—dc23

2011025954

Manufactured in China

LEO 10 9 8 7 6 5 4 3 2 1

4500350732

This book is dedicated to the memory of Curly Bear Wagner,

who fostered communication and understanding

among people of all cultures and races.

Contents

Acknowledgments

THIS PROJECT WAS PARTIALLY FUNDED BY A RESIDENT FELLOWSHIP OF the Cody Institute for Western American Studies (CIWAS) at the Buffalo Bill Historical Center in Cody, Wyoming.

The author gives special thanks to Dr. Kathryn Shanley, professor of Native American Studies, University of Montana, for her helpful reading of the manuscript and to the staff at the Buffalo Bill Historical Center for research assistance for this book.

In addition, the author and photographer wish to thank the following people and institutions for their help: Robert Applegate, David Dragonfly, Sandy Fraser, Dan Geiger, Diana Geiger, Faylene and Marty He Does It, Linda Hein, Darrell Kipp, Woody Kipp, Carmen Lunak, Dutch Lunak, Jerry Lunak, Joe Medicine Crow, Thom Meyers, Darrell Norman, Robert Pickering, Jodi Rave, Elliot Ward, Martin Weatherwax, and Roas Yearout, as well as the Blackfeet Nation, Buffalo Chips Indian Art, the Crow (Apsáalooke) Tribe, Cuts Wood School, Nez Perce National Historical Park, the Standing Rock Sioux Tribe, and Writing-on-Stone Provincial Park.

Author's Note

MANY OF THE ILLUSTRATIONS IN THIS BOOK ARE HISTORIC PHOTOGRAPHS taken in the early years of photography. Because the technology then was less well developed than today, these photos lack the sharpness and color of modern photography.

The first successful photograph was taken in 1827; it took eight hours of light exposure in order to form the image. Once people started experimenting, the process improved quickly, and by 1850 New York already had seventy-seven photography studios.

The process at that time, however, required very large cameras and several seconds of exposure, so their use was limited to studio portraits and to landscapes and buildings. In 1851 a new method that reduced exposure times to two or three seconds came about, but it required that the image be developed right after it was taken, making photos anywhere except in or near a studio impractical.

In 1871 the invention of a process that didn't require instant development advanced the field of photography, but it still required fragile glass plates and complex chemistry. Then, in 1884, George Eastman developed photographic film. Finally, photos taken out of doors in remote places and then developed later became much more practical.

Several old photos in the book are by a famous photographer of native life, Edward S. Curtis. In 1906, Curtis began a project to capture traditional Native American life before it disappeared. He traveled across North America, taking more than 40,000 photographs of more than eighty tribes. His photos, even though often specially posed for his camera, visually capture these lost ways of life.

For decades, only black-and-white photographs could be practically made. Adding color to black-and-white images became popular. In this book are a number of photos documenting traditional Blackfeet Indian life in the early twentieth century by Walter McClintock. These were part of a set of images colorized under his supervision to be sold as lantern slide sets. In the early twentieth century, people were fascinated by Indians, and they could buy McClintock's sets and project them onto screens to get glimpses of Indian life.

Thanks to photographers like Curtis and McClintock, as well as others whose work appears in this book, we can at least attempt to imagine the lives and lifestyles of native peoples before white culture forced radical changes upon them.

Prologue

THE HUNTER SCANNED THE HERD, LOOKING FOR A CHOICE BUFFALO that would provide meat for his family and that also had a healthy, thick coat that would make a warm winter robe. He zeroed in on a powerful bull, lightly tapped his heels on the flanks of his horse, and leaned forward.

He knew his mount would serve him well — he had trained it to respond to the smallest changes in pressure from his legs and to the messages he gave with his feet. He had painted arrows for swiftness on his horse's legs, and buffalo tracks on its rump to insure good hunting. His horse's eyes were encircled in red to sharpen its eyesight, and its tail was tied with eagle feathers to bring him speed.

Working together, hunter and horse raced to cut the bull from the herd and galloped close up on its left side. As his mount matched the bull stride for stride, the hunter pulled an arrow from his quiver and notched it on his bow. His horse needed no guidance now — it galloped steadily at the buffalo's side, just in back of the head, so the hunter could aim for the crucial spot

behind the rib cage. An arrow striking there would pierce the buffalo's lungs, dooming it.

As the arrow flew, the horse heard the twang of the bowstring and veered quickly away as the buffalo stumbled toward horse and rider. The bull fell, blood streaming from its mouth. Hunter and horse circled around, then stopped and waited for the prey to gasp its last breath.

Plains Indian life wasn't always like this, however. For thousands of years, native peoples who ventured onto the plains had no horses, and their lives were radically different from what they became after they got horses.

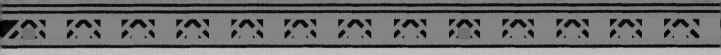

Chapter One
Living in the Dog Days

THERE was a time when an enormous carpet of grassland swept across the center of North America, from near the Rocky Mountains in the West to the edges of the eastern forests and from the plains of Canada southward deep into Texas. In this vast prairie region, few trees grew, except along the beds of the rivers and streams that carved their way through the landscape.

The prairie can be a harsh environment, punishing its inhabitants with strong winds, blazing hot summers, violent storms, and frigid winters. Despite these extremes, the prairies were home to abundant animal life. Huge herds of buffalo, also called bison, roamed there, along with deer, pronghorn, elk, wolves, and others.

The prairie stretches as far as the eye can see in every direction.

A variety of peoples also took up residence around the plains over thousands of years—hunting, fishing, and gathering plants that grew on the prairies. Some also planted food, such as the "three sisters"—beans, corn, and squash. We imagine those people mounted on swift horses, hunting buffalo or grouped at the top of a hillside, searching the horizon for enemies. But for most of their time in America, the Indians had no horses, and life could be difficult.

Helpful Dogs

When the Indians traveled in search of game, they moved camp often and had to carry their possessions with them. They harnessed their only animal helper, the dog, to load carriers called travois. Two slender poles were crossed over the dog's shoulders and bound together with leather thongs. A broad strap that looped around the dog's chest had thongs that were tied where the travois poles crossed. Behind the animal, a support tied between the poles carried the load, and the ends of the poles dragged along the ground.

Among some peoples, such as the Blackfeet, Cree, and Hidatsa, the dogs belonged to the women, who were in charge of packing up camp and moving. The women spent about four days training their dogs. They began with an empty travois, then gradually increased the load.

For thousands of years, the dog was the only companion animal of the Plains Indians.
DeGolyer Library, Southern Methodist University, Dallas, TX, AG 1982.0102

Hunting the Buffalo

Along the northwestern edge of the plains, ancestors of the modern Blackfoot (Canada) and Blackfeet (United States) Indians ventured onto the prairie from spring through autumn, depending largely on the buffalo for food, clothing, and materials for making tools. Farther south, ancestors of the Apache grew corn on the southwestern plains. On the prairies' eastern edges, farming tribes such as the Mandan and Hidatsa also hunted buffalo, as did other tribes.

Buffalo are very big, dangerous animals.

Buffalo hunting on foot was dangerous and challenging work. One method involved setting the travois on end in a semicircle and tying them securely together to form a fence near a herd of grazing buffalo. The men would then sneak up behind the herd and startle the buffalo. Women and dogs hidden behind the fence near the opening would yell or bark, which made the buffalo run into the trap formed by the fence. The men would attack the cornered buffalo with spears.

The most effective way to harvest buffalo before the horse arrived was to drive them over cliffs like this one in what is now Alberta, Canada.

Another hunting method required more people. In areas such as the northern plains, tribal bands would gather together in autumn near special cliffs called *pishkin*. In the Blackfeet tradition, when the constellation that we call the Pleiades today appeared in the sky, it was time to travel to meet at the buffalo jump.

The people cooperated in driving buffalo herds over the cliffs, butchering them, and drying the meat for winter. They used every part of the buffalo that they could, curing the hides to make blankets and clothing and tipi covers and harvesting the bones, hooves, and horns for making tools. They used the bladders and intestines for storing food and water. Little was wasted.

Life on the Prairie

While out on the prairies, the people lived in their tipis. A circle of poles leaning toward the center was lashed together where they met. Buffalo hides sewn together formed the walls, and stones anchored the edges of the tipi. The stones were left for future use, and many can still be seen today at former Indian campsites.

Even though travel was difficult, the tribes traded with one another and with tribes living beyond the prairie borders. Buffalo fat was traded with northwest coast tribes for shells and smoked salmon. Tribes far inland used shells from the sea to decorate their

Tipis provided shelter from the elements, and a fire in the center gave warmth. PHOTO BY WALTER MCCLINTOCK, YALE COLLECTION OF WESTERN AMERICANA, BEINECKE RARE BOOK AND MANUSCRIPT LIBRARY, 1050358

Over the centuries Native Americans recorded events in their lives on rocks in special locations along their travel routes. This image of warriors standing behind their shields, thought to be more than a thousand years old, is from Writing-on-Stone Provincial Park in Alberta, Canada.

clothing. Materials from hundreds of miles away—pipestone from Minnesota to the north, obsidian for arrowheads from the Rocky Mountains to the west, and Pueblo pottery from the southwest, for example—all found use among the Wichita Indians in central Kansas.

During the winter the Plains Indians found shelter in wooded valleys.

For hundreds of years the lives of the Plains Indians changed little. They spent winters in forests or river valleys, protected from the worst that the season had to offer, and ventured onto the grasslands in summer to hunt. But everything changed after Columbus found the Americas in 1492.

Chapter Two
The Miraculous Horse

SOON after Columbus's arrival, Spain began sending explorers to look for gold and other treasures and to conquer the native people. Hernando Cortés, who landed in Mexico in 1519, was the first to bring horses. Other explorers followed, bringing more and more of these animals.

The Spaniards realized how important horses were in their pursuit of subduing native people. Pedro de Castañeda de Nájera wrote in 1540:

> Horses are the most necessary things in the new country
>
> because they frighten the enemy most, and after God,
>
> to them belongs the victory.

Not only did horses frighten the Indians, they allowed the Spaniards to move much faster, to wear heavy protective armor, and to be high above the

ground. The Spaniards also had guns, which were unknown to the Indians.

After conquering the native people, the Spanish brought in cowboys, called vaqueros, who used horses to herd their sheep, cattle, and other livestock across the vast southern grasslands. Enslaved Indians tended the horses, thus learning how to take care of these new creatures and losing their fear of them.

Indians Embrace the Horse

Forbidden by the Spanish to ride, the Indians nevertheless observed closely how the Spanish rode and trained the horses. They could see how valuable these new animals were, and they were eager to possess them. The horse revolution started in the 1500s with the Apache, who managed to steal horses from the Spaniards' ranches around Santa Fe, New Mexico. Spanish records from 1659 describe mounted Apache raids on ranch stock. Horses brought wealth and power to the Apache, and the Comanche soon followed. Horses also escaped to live wild in the north.

In 1680 the Indians rebelled against their Spanish captors and drove them out of New Mexico. Suddenly the southwest tribes had easy access to the abundant number of horses that the Spanish left behind, and trading expanded northward. Horses also went free in New Mexico and in Texas after Spanish missions failed because of hostile Indians, drought, and disease.

By the late 1600s Indians in what is now New Mexico had horses and used them in intertribal warfare, as shown in this Segesser mural, painted on animal hide in the early 1700s. Some of the horses wear leather armor. PALACE OF THE GOVERNORS PHOTO ARCHIVES (NMHM/DCA), NEGATIVE #149796

Living wild on the vast grasslands, the horses quickly multiplied. In 1777 a missionary north of the Rio Grande in Texas wrote in his diary that the wild horses "are so abundant that their trails make the country, utterly uninhabited by people, look as if it were the most populated in the world." By 1800, perhaps two million horses roamed free over the southern plains.

One by one, from south to north, eager Indians acquired horses from other tribes and from the wild. The horse became especially vital to the cultures of the Plateau Indians and the Plains tribes. The Plateau Indians, such as the Kootenai and Nez Perce, lived along the Columbia River, from British Columbia in Canada southward into western Montana, northern Idaho, eastern Washington, and northern Oregon.

Many tribes lived on the plains. Some, such as the Blackfeet, had always made the prairies their home, while others, like the Sioux, moved onto the prairies as they acquired horses.

Imagine being a northern Plains Indian. It is the early 1700s, and you've heard about a powerful and mysterious new animal that has been acquired by tribes farther south. These people, it is said, use this creature to drag and carry heavy loads—like a powerful, giant dog. But most strangely, people ride on the animal's back.

Then one day while you are hunting, you climb a ridge and see an amazing sight below—a band of powerful-looking animals the size of elk, but with long tails and rounder bodies. Their coats are all different colors, some spotted and others coppery or black.

One rears up, tossing the long mane on his neck and calling out in a high-pitched voice like nothing you've ever heard. When he lands, his large round feet stir up the dust as he paws the ground. You can hardly believe your eyes. Are these the strange new creatures you've heard of, which other tribes have captured and tamed? One thing you know for sure, you want to get your hands on one.

A horse can drag much more weight on a travois than a dog can. PHOTO BY EDWARD CURTIS, LIBRARY OF CONGRESS

No one knows the exact dates, but the Shoshone in the southern Rocky Mountains and the Arapaho in the southeastern plains had horses by the early 1700s. Horses apparently reached the Crow through trading with the Shoshone around 1730. The Blackfeet got horses by 1750, probably from the Kootenai. Although the Spaniards brought the horses, most tribes had not yet encountered white people when the horses came to them. They got their horses from other Indians or from the wild.

A New Helper, a New Way of Life

Horses opened up a whole new life for Indians, which they eagerly embraced. Now people could travel much more quickly from place to place, speeding across the landscape instead of trudging along on foot. They could also move camp much more effectively, packing their gear onto horses and using them to pull the travois.

Most dogs could not drag more than seventy-five pounds, and they traveled about six miles a day, but horses could go much farther and drag three hundred pounds. Five horses could carry a family's belongings and supplies, including many more hides and long travois poles to make tipis two or three times the size of earlier ones. Camps could be farther apart because horses could walk faster than dogs and humans laden with goods, and people could ride the horses instead of walking. The old or sick could be carried on the horse-drawn travois.

Horse Stories

Each tribe has its own stories about how it acquired horses. One Crow story says that around 1730, a Crow war party ventured from their home in what is now southeastern Montana down into the Wind River area of present-day Wyoming and came back with a stallion. When they got home, people gathered around this amazing creature — tall as an elk, with a big head, large round hooves,

a shaggy mane and tail, and no antlers or horns. People examined this strange beast from all sides, and one man got too close to the rear end and the horse kicked him in the belly. From then on, his name was Kicked in the Belly, and his whole band became known as the Kicked in the Bellies. They keep this name today.

A Blackfeet story speaks of the first horses arriving with a small group of Kootenai Indians who appeared at a Blackfeet camp. The Kootenai men were ill, and the Blackfeet medicine man tried to help them, but they died. A woman, however, survived and married one of the Blackfeet men.

Meanwhile, the people tried to understand these new animals. First they fed them dried meat, which the dogs loved. But the horses, which they called sky dogs, refused the meat. The people threw sticks for the horses to fetch, but the horses ignored the sticks. One horse escaped, but two stayed, and the Blackfeet saw that they liked to eat grass. The Kootenai woman helped show the Blackfeet how to ride and groom the horses. The Blackfeet, like other tribes, were on their way to a life of new power and freedom of movement, unimaginable before the arrival of the horse.

Chapter Three

More Than a Hundred Years of Horse Culture

IN addition to the arrival of the horse, many other changes came to the plains during the 1700s and 1800s. The desire of white settlers for rich farmlands and the decline of buffalo east of the Mississippi forced more tribes onto the plains. For example, some Sioux were living in Minnesota forests and traveling by canoe in 1760, but by 1800 they had abandoned the forests and their canoes for lives as plains horsemen. Other Sioux were driven out by the Ojibwa tribe after the Ojibwa got guns from the French in the area of the Great Lakes. As such tribes were forced westward, a ripple effect began, with more and more tribes moving from their homes in the woodlands onto the plains, causing conflict with tribes that were already there.

Horses thrive on prairie grasslands.

The horses these tribes acquired allowed them to thrive in their new environment. The Cheyenne and Arapaho, for example, once lived east of the Missouri River and cultivated corn. After they got horses, they became plains buffalo hunters known for their horsemanship. The Kootenai and Nez Perce out west on the Columbia Plateau modified their traditional life of fishing and traveled by horseback onto the plains to hunt buffalo.

Plains Indian Horse Culture

By about 1770, all the Plains tribes from Texas into Canada and Illinois, as well as many Plateau tribes, had become horse nations. Each tribe brought its own traditions into its relationship with this new animal, but certain characteristics became universal enough that a generalized Plains Indian "culture area" developed. Some shared traits came from the necessities of life and the needs of the horses. For example, horses were fed cottonwood bark in winter, since most grass was buried deep in the snow.

Plains Indians like these Crow chiefs quickly developed a rich horse culture. Photo by Edward Curtis, Library of Congress

Horses and children, like this Blackfeet boy, got used to riding from a young age. Photo by Walter McClintock, Yale Collection of Western Americana, Beinecke Rare Book and Manuscript Library, 1050312

Horses were usually broken to ride by the time they were three years old, before they became too old to train easily. Young men generally used a lightweight pad saddle—swift buffalo hunters and warriors needed to avoid overburdening their horses, and they also needed to be able to dismount easily. Women, on the other hand, used saddles with wooden frames that were high in front and in back. A woman would not be galloping at a high speed, and she might be carrying an infant or hanging items on the saddle when moving camp. Other practices just made sense: young boys were usually in charge of horse care, as girls were busy helping the women and men were occupied with hunting and fighting.

Horses made buffalo hunting much easier, since a man on horseback could easily run down a buffalo when riding his specially trained horse, called a buffalo runner. The abilities of both horse and rider during the hunt were extraordinary. The mounts were taught to respond to cues the rider gave with his legs and his feet rather than with the reins. The hunters galloped into a

Artist Charles M. Russell was fascinated by the buffalo hunt and painted many images of it.
C.M. RUSSELL MUSEUM, GREAT FALLS, MONTANA

buffalo herd, frightening their prey. As the buffalo started to run, each hunter singled out one animal and raced alongside, aiming his arrow just behind the buffalo's last rib or between two forward ribs as the animal's chest expanded in a breath, which widened the space between ribs so that the arrow could go right to the animal's lungs.

Buffalo hunting involved vital teamwork. The horse needed to use its own judgment as to how fast to run and how close it dared get to the buffalo, while the rider had to steady his bow or lance while galloping full tilt across the uneven surface of the prairie. Trust between horse and rider had to be complete.

An Indian artist long ago captured the buffalo hunt in this image from Writing-on-Stone Provincial Park.

Indians had various ways of gentling their horses. A horse whisperer talked softly in a low voice to calm the animal, then gradually got it used to touch by running his hands over its whole body, ending on its legs. This helped get the horse used to the human touch. Then the trainer would press on the horse's back, gradually putting more and more weight there and finally mounting. When trained this way, horses rarely bucked.

Blackfeet and others used a different method, leading the horse into standing water up to its belly, then mounting. The horse couldn't buck in that situation and soon got used to the person on its back.

The Value of Horses

Across the plains, the horse rapidly became the most valuable possession of the people. It was their measure of wealth, and horse stealing became an honored art among Plains tribes. A poor man could increase his wealth and status quickly by successfully stealing horses. After a successful raid, a Teton Sioux usually gave some of the horses to the women in his family. A man named Two Shields sang this song, which honors the tradition:

horses

come outside

I am bringing back

older sister

come outside

and

older sister

you may catch one of them

In the 1800s, Indian men who had been taken captive by whites were sometimes given blank notebooks in which they drew images of their lives before captivity, called Ledger Art. Here, the artist (Lakota or Cheyenne) depicts a successful horse-stealing raid. NATIONAL ANTHROPOLOGICAL ARCHIVES, SMITHSONIAN INSTITUTION, NAA INV 11010800

the sioux Indian runs away with the crows horses

Blackfeet tipis at sunset. Photo by Walter McClintock, Yale Collection of Western Americana, Beinecke Rare Book and Manuscript Library

Because of the ever-present danger of horse-stealing raids, Indians kept their highly trained buffalo runners and warhorses within the village itself, even inside their dwellings. The Mandan, who lived in earthen lodges in their villages, would fence off part of the lodge interior to keep a valued buffalo runner or warhorse safe. Untrained or less valuable horses were left to graze on the outlying prairie close to camp.

The images on the war lodge tipi of the South Peigan (Blackfeet) Bear Chief depict dozens of battles and horse raids carried out by him and others. PHOTO BY WALTER MCCLINTOCK, YALE COLLECTION OF WESTERN AMERICANA, BEINECKE RARE BOOK AND MANUSCRIPT LIBRARY, 1048603

A horse raid had to be carefully planned. Sometimes Blackfeet raiders would walk for two weeks into Crow country, wearing out two pairs of mocassins on the way, so their presence would be harder to detect than if they traveled on horseback. They stayed hidden nearby for days, secretly making friends with the camp dogs by feeding them so they wouldn't alert the camp by barking when the raid was launched.

A raider would, of course, try to liberate the best buffalo runners and warhorses. After sneaking quietly into the camp, he would cut the rope that tied a horse, scramble onto its back, and gallop away, driving off some of the lesser mounts as well.

Indians as Horsemen

Warfare among the tribes and between Indians and whites became inevitable on the prairies as eastern tribes were forced west by white settlement, putting pressure on the Plains tribes, and the U.S. Army battled the Indians who resisted whites taking over their territory. Some tribes, such as the Comanche, who were among the first to acquire horses, and the Blackfeet, whose ancestors had roamed the prairies for thousands of years, became especially feared warriors.

Bravery in battle as well as in horse stealing was highly honored. Killing an enemy wasn't necessarily the goal. A practice called "counting coup" showed greater bravery, for it required the warrior to touch his enemy, alive, with the tip of his lance, his bow,

TOP: The Comanche were especially agile horsemen, able to slide over to the side of their mounts to protect themselves as they shot arrows at their enemies. *COMANCHE FEATS OF HORSEMANSHIP* BY GEORGE CATLIN, 1834–1835, SMITHSONIAN AMERICAN ART MUSEUM, WASHINGTON, D.C./ART RESOURCE, NEW YORK

BOTTOM: In this Ledger Art drawing, a Cheyenne warrior is counting coup on his enemy using his lance. NATIONAL ANTHROPOLOGICAL ARCHIVES, SMITHSONIAN INSTITUTION, NAA INV 08666200

Edward Curtis was a photographer who made documenting the American Indians his life's work. This photo shows a Nez Perce warrior with his coup stick. PHOTO BY EDWARD CURTIS, LIBRARY OF CONGRESS

or a special "coup stick." Warriors kept track of their coups, and those with the highest counts carried the most honor. A warrior often marked his coups with lines on the legs of his warhorse.

Keeping Track of Time

As the years passed, tribes kept track of time by choosing a key event each year to illustrate on a special buffalo hide called a winter count. The history of the band recorded there tells of trials and triumphs—battles won and lost, epidemics endured, years of bounty, and years of famine. Because of their importance, horses appear often on winter count hides.

These images were copied from a winter count by an Oglala Sioux chief named American Horse. The image of the horse being lassoed stands for the years 1811–1812, when the band caught many wild horses south of the Platte River. "AMERICAN HORSE" WINTER COUNT, NATIONAL ANTHROPOLOGICAL ARCHIVES, SMITHSONIAN INSTITUTION, INV 08634000

Lakota artist Sam Two Kills makes a copy of the "Big Missouri" winter count on a buffalo robe.
"Big Missouri" winter count by Sam Two Kills, Nebraska State Historical Society, RG2969

The Gift Horse

Valuable possessions, horses also became common gifts for special occasions. A man would give horses to his future in-laws, and a boy might be given a horse when he reached a milestone in his life, such as killing his first buffalo. A gift of horses could help raise the status of both the giver and those to whom the horses were given.

Today, too, horses are often given as gifts within the tribes. Special gatherings called giveaways are still held by many tribes to honor a soldier returning from war or a student graduating from school. At such gatherings, horses can be favorite presents.

A proud Crow father tells how one Christmas, when his three daughters and their husbands came to help celebrate, he told his sons-in-law to look under the Christmas tree. There, for each, was an empty bridle. "In the spring," he told them, "go to my pasture and pick out the horse you want from my herd. It is my gift to you for being such good husbands to my daughters."

Chapter Four

Horses and the Spirit

IMAGINE being a young Plains Indian, living in a tipi in a small prairie encampment. You need to lift the tipi flap and bend over to enter your circular home. The walls are made of buffalo hide, strong but not soundproof, so you can hear everything going on outside—the wind through the grass, the plodding of horses' hooves, the voices of young children playing and mothers scolding. You have no electricity and are warmed by the fire in the center of the tipi, the smoke going up through the opening at the top. There are no individual rooms, just areas set aside for eating and sleeping.

When you go outside, you are on the prairie—there are no streets, no sidewalks, no buildings or traffic, just the tipis, the horses, and the land. Every

A Blackfeet encampment. PHOTO BY WALTER MCCLINTOCK, YALE COLLECTION OF WESTERN AMERICANA, BEINECKE RARE BOOK AND MANUSCRIPT LIBRARY, 1046884

day you are close to nature. The weather can change quickly and become violent, with tornadoes, powerful lightning storms, and blizzards. Summer means blazing heat and winter means numbing cold, with only the walls of your tipi to separate you from the forces of nature. You live close to the earth, hearing the sounds and smelling the aromas of nature every day.

This closeness to nature fostered a strong connection of Indian peoples to the animals. As the Southern Cheyenne writer W. Richard West, Jr., wrote:

> *Indians have traditionally regarded the animals in our lives as fellow creatures with whom we share a common destiny. Whereas for many non-Natives, an animal can sometimes be little more than a "beast of burden" or a depersonalized food source, for Native people, that animal is soul mate, friend, brother.*

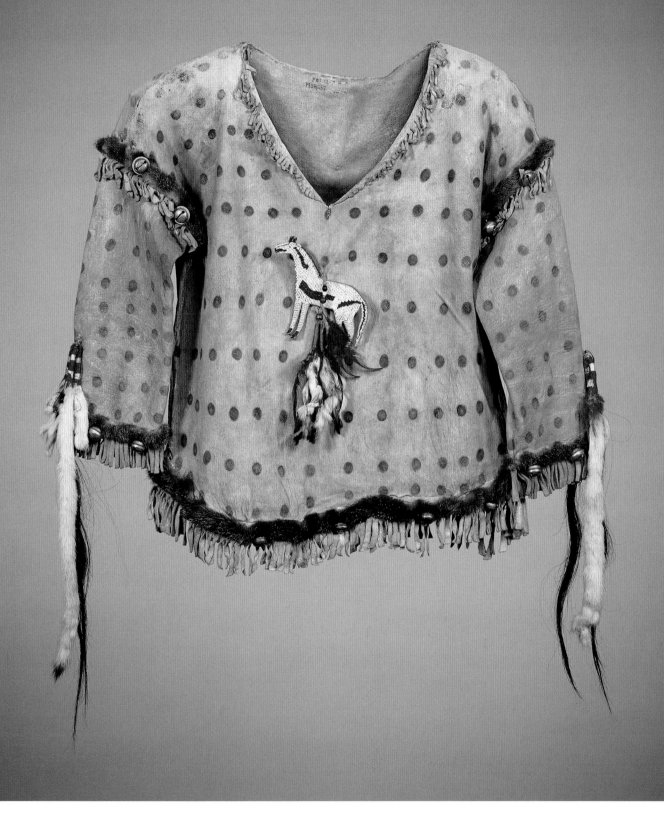

This Sun Dance shirt from about 1865 bears a beaded horse effigy, giving the wearer horse medicine power.

The Powerful Horse

To the Plains Indians, animals had special powers because they could survive in the wild on their own, without fire and without protective lodging. While humans come into the world helpless and needing to be taught, animals have inborn knowledge about

In this drawing by a Kiowa artist, the zigzags on the horse symbolize the lightning power associated with horses. National Anthropological Archives, Smithsonian Institution, NAA INV 08547626

survival. The powers of animals could be accessed by people through fasting and visions. Symbols of animals, as well as the animals themselves—or symbols of the elements of nature—could bring protection, good luck, or success in challenging situations such as war and the hunt.

A young man would leave camp alone, climb a mountain, and stay there without food or water for days, hoping the spirit of an animal would come to him in a dream or a vision. That animal would become his spirit helper. Dreams and visions obtained in this way were interpreted with the help of a medicine person.

Horses quickly became an essential part of the spiritual lives of the Plains tribes because of the power, beauty, and importance of these animals. While many tribes used a name that meant "elk dog" for horses, some other names had a more spiritual meaning. For example, the Dakota word for horse, *s'unkawakan,* could be translated as "great mysterious dog" or "sacred dog."

Medicine People

Individuals with special spiritual capacity, commonly referred to as medicine people, often received their gifts through animals, and "horse medicine" was particularly powerful among the Plains tribes. A man with horse medicine could be blessed with the strength and agility of the horse. He might be especially good at finding lost horses or at stealing horses. He would have special horse songs to sing and special horse ceremonies to carry out.

Horse medicine was especially powerful among the tribes of the Blackfoot and Blackfeet, who had societies, songs, and dances to honor horses.

Medicine people, usually men, were in charge of caring for special packages of important power symbols, called medicine bundles. Some bundles were personal to one man, while others were significant to the whole band or tribe. The sacred Thunder Pipe Bundle of the Blackfeet was carried by a horse reserved for this specific purpose. The horse was painted with a red stripe on its forehead and down its nose. Its mane and tail were also painted red, and zigzags and red dots decorated its body and neck. The woman who led this horse was considered to be the most honored in all the tribe.

Realms of Spirit and Life

Although each Plains tribe had its own variations on how the world was put together, the general basis for spirituality was similar among the tribes. The world consisted of three realms: the upper realm of sky, the middle region of earth and the living things that walked upon it, and the underground and water spirits. The idea that air and water spirits complemented each other, even though they were often in conflict, existed across the West, from the Dakotas to British Columbia.

The worlds of sky and water were always at war, with the earth in the middle. The sun and moon, along with the thunderbird—

which sent powerful bolts of lightning from the sky—provided the energy to control the seasons and night and day. Indian stories from the Crow and Blackfeet say that the horse came out of the water. Several versions of this story exist, a common theme being a poor young boy traveling to a lake where he meets an underwater chief who helps him by giving him the gift of horses.

Thunder and lightning are awesome powers on the wide-open prairie. In the stories, horses carried the power of the thunderbird, which brought about lightning and thunder by flapping its wings and flashing its eyes. When horses run, their hooves pound the ground, creating a sound like that of thunder.

This painting of a horse dance from about 1885 by the Lakota artist Sam Two Kills shows horses wearing buffalo horns and painted with lightning marks and spots representing hail. Both the front horse and its rider are wearing buffalo masks and leggings. *An Indian Horse Dance* by Sam Two Kills, THE ONLINE COLLECTION OF C. SZWEDZICKI: THE NORTH AMERICAN INDIAN WORKS, UNIVERSITY OF CINCINNATI LIBRARIES

Crow Horse Mask

Everything on this Crow horse mask from the late 1800s meant something to the warrior who used it. To the Indians, the images painted on their animals or worked into their clothing and horse gear were much more than decoration; they had the power to influence reality. The red and yellow dots represent hail, and the yellow lines probably mean wind. If you look closely, you can see that the dots and lines run in different directions on the two sides of the mask, suggesting a message to the enemy: You can't hide; wherever you seek shelter, the rain and hail can get to you.

The bright metal balls around the eyeholes reflected the sun's rays, as if lightning power were flashing from the horse's eyes and attacking the enemy. Their roundness could be another symbol for balls of hail.

The symbolic buffalo horns above the eyes are accented by bits of bird feather fluff dyed red, and feathers from magpies and golden eagles adorn the forehead, while great horned owl feathers encircle the horns. Each of these birds probably represents a different valued trait — owls can see in the dark, magpies are especially intelligent, and eagles have the broad view and can see the big picture rather than just the details.

Horse Power

Horses were often painted before a battle or a hunt to provide them with power and protection. Zigzags on the neck and legs stood for lightning, and spots or upside-down *U*'s on the body indicated hail. Arrows drawn in a line helped bring victory. Arrowheads painted on the hooves helped make the horse fast and nimble.

This Charles M. Russell painting, *Medicine Horse,* shows a horse painted with the image of a man on its chest, a sign that the horse ran down a man in battle. MEDICINE HORSE BY CHARLES M. RUSSELL, 1912 OIL ON BOARD, C.M. RUSSELL MUSEUM, GREAT FALLS, MONTANA

Some horse masks were made of hide and horns, such as those worn by two of the horses in this photo of Sioux from around 1895. Notice the lightning lines without zigzags painted on the horse in front. LIBRARY OF CONGRESS, LC-USZ62-110873

An image of the horns of the fastest runner on the plains — the pronghorn — could make a horse swift, and a dragonfly image might help a horse survive in battle. Eyes and nostrils were circled in red to sharpen the animal's vision and give it an enhanced sense of smell. Eagle feathers, a symbol of thunder power, were often tied onto a horse's tail.

A tradition that probably derived from the protective metal armor the Spanish used on their horses' heads is the horse mask, found in tribes from the Mandan to the Cheyenne, the Sioux to the Blackfeet, and westward to the Salish and Plateau tribes such as the Nez Perce. Horse masks were used to give horses special powers. Masks made from buffalo hide and topped with buffalo horns might aid a horse in the hunt or give it the toughness of the buffalo in war. Some horse masks have eyeholes surrounded by lightning zigzags or other symbols of power and protection.

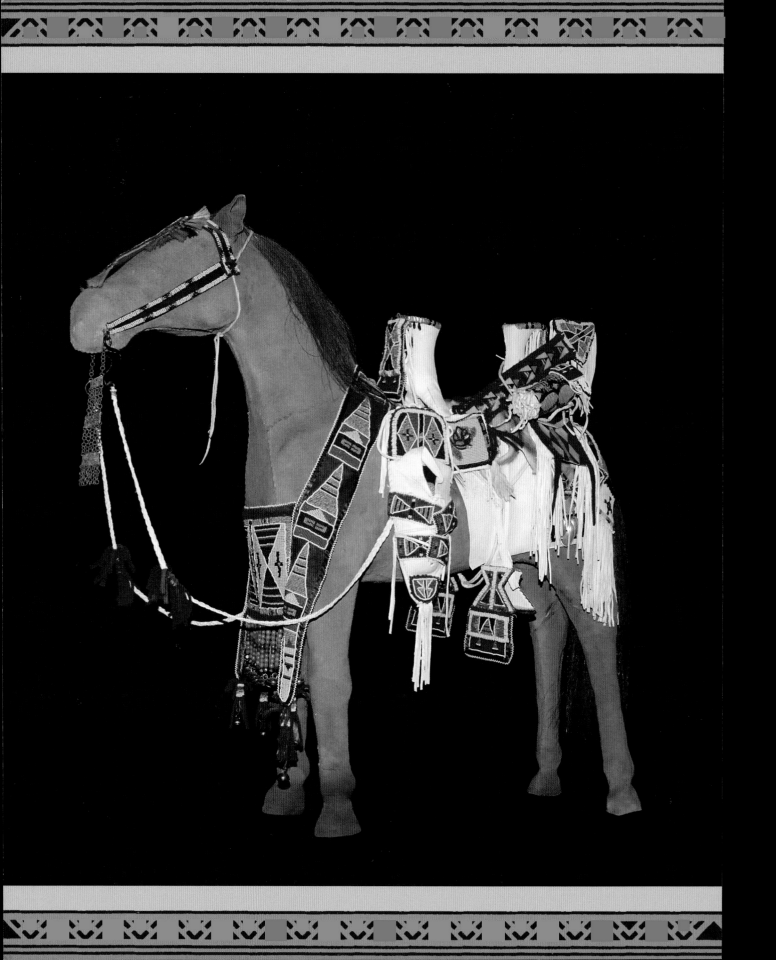

Chapter Five

Horse Gear
and Decoration

BEFORE horses arrived, Indian warriors fought on foot. The men made their own shields for warfare from the especially thick hide on the buffalo's neck. A few women also became warriors and were treated as if they were men. Ancient rock art shows that these shields were about three feet in diameter. But such large shields were impossible to manipulate on horseback, so the shields became smaller, about eighteen inches in diameter. The men painted their shields with such symbols as buffalo, the sun, or the thunderbird, which would give them power and protect them in battle. Horses might be painted in blue on a shield to show their connection to sky powers.

Indian Creativity

As nomads who moved camp often, Plains Indians needed carrying cases for their goods. The parfleche was the Indian equivalent of a storage bag or suitcase. To make a parfleche, a woman staked out a damp buffalo hide, with the hair facing the ground. She used willow sticks to measure and mark out a pair of parfleches on the hide, one for each side of a horse. Then she sketched geometric designs on the front and sides of the case. After outlining the sections of the design with one color, she filled in the areas with different colors. The artist would either mix the paint with hot water so it sank into the hide, permanently dyeing it, or she would cover the painted area with glue made by boiling a beaver tail. After the paint dried, she turned the hide over and scraped off the hair with a rock, leaving a whitish surface that showed off the colors on the other side. Then she cut out each parfleche with a sharp knife, folded each into an envelope, and used a hot rod for making holes for ties.

Indians have always enjoyed bringing beauty into their everyday and ceremonial lives, and horses provide them with a variety of items to decorate. In the past, the patterns and

A Blackfeet girl makes parfleches. PHOTO BY WALTER McCLINTOCK, YALE COLLECTION OF WESTERN AMERICANA, BEINECKE RARE BOOK AND MANUSCRIPT LIBRARY, 1046870

Osage horse mirror made around 1880. BUFFALO CHIPS, BILLINGS, MONTANA

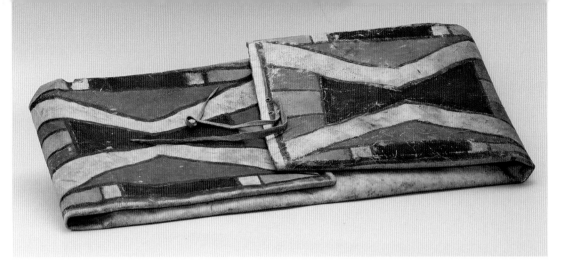

A parfleche from the Nez Perce tribe. National Park Service, Nez Perce National Historical Park, NEPE184_Bag

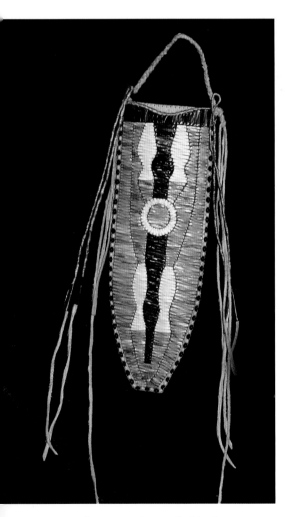

A Hidatsa-Mandan quilled knife case.
Case artist, Honza Podemeny

images that decorated horses and horse gear usually had special meanings. People continue these ways, but not as many people seek visions and dreams as they once did. But even today tipis and horses at Indian gatherings may be decorated by special symbolic designs. Each tribe developed its own favorite themes and designs, so that one could recognize the tribal identity of an encampment even from a distance.

Before the arrival of European traders, clothing, bags, and horse gear were decorated using quillwork. The sharp black tips of porcupine quills were cut off, and the quills were softened and dyed using natural dyes from plants. Quillwork is time-consuming labor, and when traders began bringing beads, many Indians started using them instead to decorate their creations. The first beads brought by white traders were called pony beads because they were brought in by pony pack trains. These beads were relatively large and somewhat irregular. They came in only a few colors, blue being the most common. Later, smaller beads, called seed beads because of their size, became very popular for their different colors and the possibilities that their small size created for intricate designs.

Indian beadwork uses many patterns, today as in the past. Floral designs, introduced by the Cree and Ojibwa, have become widely used. Northern tribes such as the Assiniboin and Gros Ventre, and especially the Blackfeet, have favored geometric checkerboard designs using squares and triangles. Among the Crow, a popular pattern for the decorative beaded ornament on a horse's forehead is the morning star design, which has a circle in the center with

Nez Perce gauntlets decorated with a horse design. National Park Service, Nez Perce National Historical Park, NEPE8990_Gauntlets

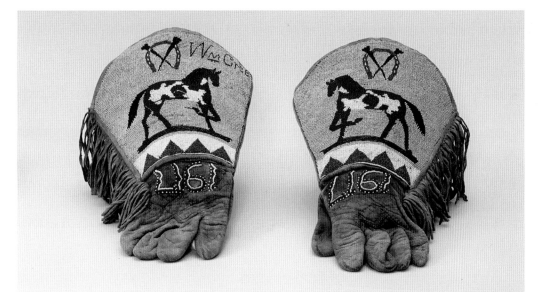

four arms extending outward. When American flags are incorporated into a pattern, it usually means that the user is a war veteran or that there is a veteran in the family.

Southern tribes such as the Kiowa, Comanche, Arapaho, and Pawnee lived south of the range of porcupines, so they didn't have a tradition of quillwork designs. Their clothing and possessions are more likely to be decorated by narrow beadwork edging, paint, and leather fringes.

Indian Horse Gear

Much Indian horse gear is similar to that of the Spaniards. When the Lewis and Clark expedition passed through the American West in 1805, they spent a few days with the Shoshone along what is now the border between Idaho and Montana. In his journal, Meriwether Lewis wrote that the men wore armor made of many folds of antelope skin held together with glue and sand, which they also put on their horses. (The Spanish and their horses wore

Young men often rode using a simple pad saddle. This one is beautifully decorated with beadwork.

armor made of metal.) But leather armor, however thick, could not stop bullets, so when rifles became common among the tribes, horse armor disappeared.

The wood-framed saddles used by Shoshone women and old men described by Lewis had leather-covered wooden stirrups and were similar to the pack saddles used by the Spanish. That style, with a rawhide-covered wooden frame that has a high front, called the cantle, and a high back, called the pommel, is still used today in parades and celebrations, often with beautifully beaded decorations.

Lewis also described the typical horse gear of the tribe. Instead of a bridle, the Shoshone used a halter made of rawhide or braided buffalo hair. It was tied around the horse's neck, then up to the animal's lower jaw and looped through the mouth. The rest of the rope was kept long so that it dragged on the ground even while horse and rider galloped full speed. Apparently the horses didn't trip over the trailing ropes.

Lewis wrote that young Shoshone men rode either bareback or on a simple leather pad saddle that was stuffed with hair and held in place with a leather thong around the horse's belly. Men in other tribes also used pad saddles, sometimes with stirrups that helped the rider remain balanced on the horse. The corners of the saddle and the stirrups were often decorated with beadwork. Today, many Plains Indian horsemen use typical western saddles.

Horse gear both past and present includes many other items that can be decorated. Indians may use a crupper—a strap that passes from the saddle around

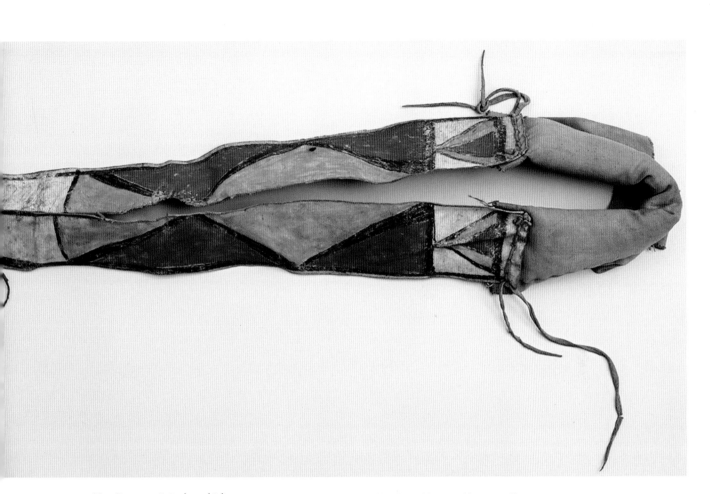

Nez Perce painted rawhide crupper. NATIONAL PARK SERVICE, NEZ PERCE NATIONAL HISTORICAL PARK, NEPE2239_CRUPPER

the rear of the horse to keep the saddle from moving forward—and a martingale. One type of martingale passes around the horse's chest and keeps the saddle from slipping backward. Another type is a decorative loose collar that hangs around the horse's neck. All of these items are often adorned with colorful beadwork. Crow martingale patterns have triangles, like a mountain range, while those from Plateau tribes such as the Nez Perce feature narrow, slashlike marks.

Chapter Six
Tragedies Strike

MANY people date the last battle of the Indian wars with the Wounded Knee Massacre in December of 1890, which was more a senseless slaughter than a battle. At the time, hundreds of Indians were camped on the Pine Ridge Reservation of South Dakota, near Wounded Knee Creek. The tension between soldiers sent to guard the area and the Indians ran high. The Ghost Dance, a new religious movement among the Lakota, only added to the soldiers' fears, as some Ghost Dance leaders predicted that the white man would soon be gone from the plains.

The combination of desperate, starving Indians and nervous soldiers assigned to disarm them resulted in a terrible slaughter of more than 150 Indian men, women, and children from the band of Lakota Chief Big Foot.

White and Indian Conflict

The arrival of white people in North America had brought trouble right from the start. Along with the fur trade came epidemics of smallpox, measles, and other diseases that devastated tribes across the continent. For example, in 1781 a terrible smallpox epidemic hit the Mandan, natives of what is now North Dakota. The epidemic reduced their population from as many as nine villages to just two. Having lost eighty percent or more of their population, the tribe moved north to be near the Hidatsa at the mouth of the Knife River. The Mandan were not alone. Up to half of the Plains Indians died from smallpox between 1779 and 1781. Other epidemics hit various tribes in 1801–02, 1816–17, and again in 1837 as trade with whites expanded, but many of those who died had never even seen a white man. Along with the epidemics came increasing pressure from white travelers and settlers.

This photo of an unidentified Plains Indian family during the 1800s shows the poverty that came to these people with the arrival of the whites. Photo by Alexander Gardner, Ft. Laramie National Anthropological Archives, Smithsonian Institution, NAA INV 01601908

White Settlement Becomes a Threat

Even so, Indians on the Great Plains strengthened their cultures and expanded their hunting grounds into the 1800s, largely through the advantages brought to them by horses. By the mid-1800s, however, continued conflict between the whites and Indians

After the Indians were reduced to reservation life, they had to depend on the government for meager food rations. Here, Sioux women await the arrival of the rations. PHOTO BY C. G. MORLEDGE, DENVER PUBLIC LIBRARY, WESTERN HISTORY COLLECTION, X31305

became inevitable. The discovery of gold in Colorado and California brought thousands of adventurers across the middle of the Great Plains, right through traditional tribal hunting grounds, in search of treasure. The first railroad across North America was completed in 1869. The Indians were clearly in the way of the settlers' westward expansion, and the nomadic, buffalo-hunting way of life among the tribes could not continue. The Plains Indian way of life that depended on horses was doomed.

As trouble brewed on the plains, Indians were being forced from the east and placed on reservations to the west. The original idea behind putting Indians on reservations was to give them land to settle on while clearing the way for white travelers and settlers across the plains. The Indians had to depend on government rations for food, as the buffalo were almost gone, but the government often cut the rations in attempts to force the Indians to feed themselves by farming. Most of the tribes were not familiar with farming methods, and much reservation land was not suitable for farming. The result was desperate hunger among the Indians.

Broken treaties and broken promises by the government plagued Indians who had peacefully agreed to be moved to reservations. European American settlers in general had little sympathy for the Indians' plight. In Minnesota, one storekeeper brushed them off by saying, "If they are hungry, let them eat grass." Whenever the Indians tried to regain their land in the Midwest and the West by fighting back, the U.S. Army always triumphed eventually. No one knows just how many people on both sides of the conflict, including women and children, lost their lives. Meanwhile, in the South and East, both sides in the Civil War courted tribes to be their allies, increasing violence and distrust.

The U.S. Army and bounty hunters almost wiped out the buffalo in the late 1800s.

The Custer Fight by William Herbert Dunton shows Sioux warriors during the Battle of the Little Bighorn. Notice the painting on the horses' bodies and legs. BUFFALO BILL HISTORICAL CENTER, CODY, WYOMING; GERTRUDE VANDERBILT WHITNEY TRUST FUND PURCHASE, 48.61

Things were especially bad in Colorado, where miners and settlers wanted to get rid of the Indians. In 1864 U.S. soldiers attacked a Cheyenne encampment at Sand Creek, killing every Indian they could, including women and children.

Getting Rid of the Indians

Meanwhile, the army decided that if buffalo were eliminated, the Indians could be forced into a settled life as farmers on reservations. Countless hunters targeted buffalo all across the plains, killing them by the millions from horseback and from the windows of trains. Often only the hides or the tongues, considered a delicacy, were taken. Buffalo Bill Cody, a famous soldier and showtime personality of the time, claimed to have killed 4,280 buffalo in a year and a half, once killing forty-eight in just fifty minutes. In those times, this was considered a proud accomplishment.

The latter part of the nineteenth century saw a series of tragic events—army attacks on Indian villages followed by strikes in return by the Indians, over and over again. One of the worst was the Battle of the Washita, in which General George Armstrong Custer attacked a friendly Cheyenne village, killing most of the Indians, including women and children, and shooting all the Indians' horses.

Many bands of the Sioux tribe, including the Brulé, were camped at Pine Ridge when the army massacre occurred. Photo by John C. H. Grabill, Library of Congress, LC-DIG-ppmsc-02508

After Big Foot's band was decimated, it became clear that the Indians had no chance against the hundreds of soldiers of the U.S. Army. PHOTO BY JOHN C. H. GRABILL, DENVER PUBLIC LIBRARY, WESTERN HISTORY COLLECTION, NS 291

The authorities believed that Indians without horses would be easier to control, but this raid on a friendly village only brought on more Indian attacks.

After the Battle of the Washita, Custer visited a Cheyenne encampment and sealed his peace with the tribe by smoking a sacred peace pipe, swearing he would not fight the tribe again. But Custer's vow was not sincere. Instead, in 1876 he and his men attacked an encampment of Northern Cheyenne and several Lakota Sioux bands in the famous Battle of the Little Bighorn. Custer and his men were wiped out.

The Battle of the Little Bighorn made the American army even more determined than before to control the native peoples. Conflict continued, climaxing in the Wounded Knee Massacre, which made it clear that the traditional Indian way of life was finished.

Chapter Seven
Life Between Two Worlds

FOR almost four hundred years whites and Indians fought over the lands of North America. By the end of the nineteenth century the whites occupied land all the way from the Atlantic Ocean to the Pacific, and the Indians had been corralled onto reservations that consisted of a small fraction of their original lands. The buffalo were gone, and the land was now divided up into mostly privately owned bits and pieces. The Indians had to find new ways of living.

Getting Rid of Horses

As tribe after tribe, decimated by disease and without game to hunt, was forced to give up its land, the whites also deprived them of their horses. The government decided that if the horses were gone, the Indians

Horses on the Blackfeet Reservation.

would adapt to reservation life more easily. For example, when a large number of Kiowa and Comanche Indians surrendered in 1875, their 3,500 or so horses were taken away. Some were shot, and others were given to military scouts. About 1,600 were sold, and the profits were used to buy sheep and goats, with the idea that these hunters of the plains could easily be turned into settled herders.

Not only were most of their horses removed, but Indians on reservations were also forbidden to hunt, to wear traditional clothing, or to sing and dance their traditional music. They could not carry out their traditional ceremonies such as the Sun Dance, an especially important annual event that brought people together every summer for ceremony, renewing friendships, and social networking.

A big problem for the Indians was how to provide for their families on the reservations. If they still had horses and wanted to sell some, they were allowed to sell only to people with special licenses—whites who often took advantage of them. They were supposed to become farmers, but successful farming requires a great deal of knowledge, good soil, a variety of tools, and a settled lifestyle.

Richard Pratt and the Carlisle School

In 1875 an army captain named Richard Pratt was assigned the duty of escorting a group of Plains Indian prisoners, many of whom were war chiefs, from Kansas all the way to Fort Marion in Florida, where they were to be held. The warriors came from various tribes,

This Ledger Art drawing was made by Etahdleuh, one of the Fort Marion artists, in 1880. National Anthropological Archives, Smithsonian Institution, NAA INV 08517800

including Kiowa, Comanche, Apache, and Cheyenne. The journey took twenty-four days, and Pratt treated the Indians well. Once in Florida, he stayed with them and worked to improve their living conditions by getting them to build wooden barracks for themselves in the fresh ocean air. Pratt trained them to become a proud military company. He gave them paper and drawing materials, and the prisoners drew vibrant pictures of Indian life, which they sold to tourists to make spending money. Most of these drawings include images of the beloved horse — that missing piece of the Indian heart and soul.

After these prisoners were freed, Pratt went on to found the Carlisle Indian Industrial School for Indian children in Pennsylvania.

A classroom at the Carlisle School. PHOTO BY FRANCES BENJAMIN JOHNSTON, 1864–1952, LIBRARY OF CONGRESS

His experience with the prisoners had strengthened his belief that Indians could be educated into a typical white man's style of life as farmers and tradespeople. From 1879 to 1918, tens of thousands of Indian children were taken from their families and enrolled at Carlisle and other boarding schools in an effort to integrate Indians into the white man's way of life.

At the boarding schools, everything possible was done to strip the children of their Indian identity. Their traditional clothing was taken away, and their hair was cut short. Indians traditionally cut their hair only during periods of mourning, so losing it was especially traumatic for the children. Luther Standing Bear, a chief of the Oglala Lakota, wrote of his childhood feelings:

> I was called out of the schoolroom, and when I went into the next room, the barber was waiting for me. He motioned for me to sit down, and then he commenced work. But when my hair was cut short, it hurt my feelings to such an extent that the tears came from my eyes. . . . Now after having had my hair cut . . . I felt that I was no more Indian, but would be an imitation of a white man.

Typically, the children would attend school in the mornings and work for white families in the afternoons, boys as farm laborers and girls as maids in the homes. They were isolated from their families and their tribes, and from horses. After receiving the equivalent of an eighth-grade education, these young people returned to their reservations, where there were no jobs for them. They had little or no knowledge of their tribes' traditions, and they felt lost.

Wild West Shows

Some adult Indians managed to make lives for themselves off the reservations, where they could make use of their skill with horses. Their horsemanship enabled some to get jobs as cowboys on ranches. Americans were very curious about Indian cultures and about the challenging times of white settlement in the "Wild West." A number of "Wild West shows" toured not only the United States but also Europe, with performances by Indians enacting Indian warfare and horsemanship.

Willie Holy Frog was an Indian who performed in Wild West shows. PHOTO BY EDWARD CURTIS, LIBRARY OF CONGRESS

Buffalo Bill's Wild West, which toured from 1883 to 1913, was the most famous of these institutions. For six months each year, the Indian performers could escape the poverty and bleakness of reservation life and display their amazing horsemanship to the world. They could wear their traditional clothing and sing their traditional songs, and they received pay for their performances.

Sometimes performers portrayed themselves as horseback Indians even

TOP: The words on this poster for Buffalo Bill's Wild West show say a lot about the attitude toward Indians at the time. LIBRARY OF CONGRESS

BOTTOM: Here is Wenona, the mysterious woman sharpshooter who claimed to be an Indian. PHOTO BY EDWARD CURTIS, LIBRARY OF CONGRESS

if their heritage was uncertain. Winsome Wenona, the Wonder Shot of the World, performed in two different Wild West shows after she had worked for Buffalo Bill under the name Lillian Smith. Was she the daughter of a Delaware lighthouse keeper or of Crazy Snake, a

Lakota chief? What mattered wasn't who she really was but that the audience thought she was an "Indian Princess" and that she could shoot better than the famous Annie Oakley.

Adapting and Celebrating

Frustrated by their failure to turn Indians into farmers, the white Indian agents on Pine Ridge and Rosebud reservations in South Dakota in the 1890s decided that it might help the Indians to become patriotic Americans if the Lakota Sioux held fairs to celebrate the Fourth of July. The tribe was delighted. July 4 was only two weeks after the traditional time for the Sun Dance, which was forbidden to the Indians at that time. Now they could get together again in early summer to renew their relationships and celebrate.

The Indian version of the celebration became a typically Indian event rather than a white man's county fair. Parades had always been popular with Indians, so a Fourth of July parade with lots of horses was fine with them. Giveaways had been a customary part of the Sun Dance, so now they were incorporated into the Independence Day celebrations. The Lakota made sure to satisfy the authorities by displaying an abundance of American flags.

A few years later, the success of similar fairs among the Navajo led the superintendent of the Crow Reservation in southeastern Montana to institute an annual fair in 1905. The idea was to encourage the Indians to become farmers and win cash prizes for the best crops. The Indians, in great need of ways to make money, en-

At the Fourth of July parade at Pine Ridge about 1905, an Oglala Lakota boy was honored to be riding this special horse that would be given away during the celebration. STATE ARCHIVES OF THE SOUTH DAKOTA STATE HISTORICAL SOCIETY, #69 FB 106

thusiastically competed. They were also allowed to help run the fairs, another opportunity for employment.

The fair became very popular. In addition to the paid work and prizes it offered, it gave Crow from all over the reservation a chance

Horses graze on the Northern Cheyenne Reservation in Montana.

to camp together and catch up with one another. Indians ran the concessions, providing yet another chance to earn some money. The events also featured horseracing, which allowed the Indians to show off the talents of their favorite animal companion.

Crow Reservation Tragedy

But the tribe soon got into more conflicts with whites. The Crow Reservation had excellent grazing land, and Crow horses thrived there, multiplying into the thousands. White ranchers had their eyes on these fine pastures and wanted to use them to raise beef cattle. The Crow were reluctant to allow this. They wanted to keep their land for their beloved horses.

The ranchers kept putting pressure on the government. Finally, in 1919, the U.S. Department of the Interior gave the Crow one year to get rid of their horses. The range needed to be rid of "worthless horses" that ate grass that could feed cattle or sheep. The government had the horses rounded up and returned those with brands to their owners. Some of the other horses were sold. But while the Indians watched helplessly, tens of thousands of horses were shot by hired white gunmen who were paid four dollars for each dead horse, and the bodies were left to rot. Riding horses that were kept near homes and the wilder ones out on the range all met their end. This slaughter devastated the Crow, who viewed horses as part of their family.

Chapter Eight
Indians and Horses Today

THROUGH the early twentieth century, Indians struggled to make lives for themselves with the limited resources they had on the reservations. Whites were in charge, and Indian desires and needs were mostly ignored.

Change began slowly in the 1930s, when President Franklin D. Roosevelt appointed John Collier, a critic of reservation law, as commissioner of Indian Affairs. Collier helped pass the Indian Reorganization Act through Congress in 1934. This law gave the tribes more power over their own affairs and ended white takeover of reservation land. The law had flaws, but it was a start.

Return of the Horses

Luckily for the Crow, one of their own, Robert Yellowtail, became superintendent of the Crow Reservation in 1934. He understood a major part of the problem for Plains tribes like the Crow:

> *Crows have always been close to horses. Without them we're sunk.*
> *Today Crows still love horses. To separate us from horses, you might*
> *as well take one of our family away. . . . Crows are like Arabs, with horses*
> *all around them, and they love them like members of their family.*

Yellowtail brought in quality stallions of several breeds, including Morgans, quarter horses, and Thoroughbreds, to help upgrade the quality of horses on the reservation. The horses multiplied once again, returning to their important roles in tribal life. As one Crow put it in 1937:

Fine horses meant everything to us Crows — they still do. It was like this: you wanted good horses for yourself, and not only that, you wanted them for your relatives too, because you want your relatives to have things as nice as you do.

A girl and her horse dressed in finery for the Crow Fair Parade. PHOTO BY DOROTHY PATENT

Sculptor Jay Laber created this striking piece, which greets people as they enter the Blackfeet Reservation.

Other Plains tribes such as the Blackfeet also raise fine horses today. Some Blackfeet have brought in Spanish mustangs, a breed with roots in the Spanish settlement of the West, while other Blackfeet breed quarter horses used in movies, such as *Hildago*. Plateau tribes have also worked to revive their horse culture, and many Nez Perce today raise the hardy Appaloosa horses they are known for.

Nowadays, although many Indians still live and work on reservations, others live far away and work in all kinds of professions as educators, doctors, and lawyers. Many carry with them a reminder of the importance of horses in their family names, such as Spotted Horse, White Horse Woman, Horse Capture, and Her Many Horses.

But wherever Indians are, horses continue to inspire the creativity of Indian people and to help them connect with their cultures. Like many other Indian artists across North America, Cree, Salish, and Shoshone painter Jaune Quick-to-See Smith feels a strong connection to horses, and exhibitions of her work are titled Horses Make a Landscape Look More Beautiful and She Paints the Horse, while Blackfeet printmaker David Dragonfly often includes horses in his creations. Blackfeet artist Jay Laber follows the Indian tradition of making use of what is available, creating powerful sculptures, often involving horses, from rusty old cars, barbed wire, and other found items.

Crow Fair Today

Horses are once again an integral part of Crow tribal life and continue to inspire traditional Crow arts. Crow Fair was suspended during World War II. When it started up again, the agricultural exhibits disappeared and the fair became an opportunity for honoring Indian life, including the importance of horses in Crow society.

Crow Fair tipis.

Skeeter He Does It rides in the parade.

Crow Fair today is a four-day festival centered around horses. About a thousand tipis stand on the grounds. Twenty thousand to thirty thousand Indians from Canada and all over the United States come to catch up with friends and family and to compete in the parade, the rodeo, and Indian dancing. Children ride bareback through the campground all day long and lead their horses to water in the river that flows through the camp. Each morning, tribal members dressed in traditional clothing parade through the camp, riding their beautifully decorated horses. Men wear long, feathered headdresses, and women dress in blouses decorated with elk teeth. A cougar hide may serve as a saddle blanket to show that the woman's husband is a hunter. A parading woman might tie her husband's shield to the pommel of her saddle. If she owns two fancy dresses, she may wear one and spread the other over the back of the horse to show it off. As one Crow woman put it, "We are show people. If we've got it, we bring it out and show it."

The parade can stretch for as long as two miles. Each Crow Fair afternoon features a rodeo with typical competitions such as bareback riding and calf roping, as well as horseracing. A favorite event is the Indian relay race in which a team consisting of one rider and three helpers compete. Riding bareback, one of the team members begins by galloping full tilt around the track. Then each racer jumps off his mount, and one of his teammates, called the catcher, grabs it. The rider scrambles atop a second horse with help from his teammates. It isn't easy to mount an excited, prancing horse and gallop down the track, and mishaps are common. The race lasts three cycles, each on a different horse, and enthusiastic cheers and whoops greet the winner.

The team roping contest.

A boy rides his horse at Crow Fair.

All afternoon, children of all ages ride their horses around the fairgrounds, often bareback. They linger at the fence, watching the rodeo events, and hold their own spontaneous races along the back stretch of the course between races. Horses are clearly once again an important part of growing up Crow.

Indian rodeo is popular across the continent. The Indian National Finals Rodeo Association, founded in 1976, sponsors competitions throughout Indian country, including some for young people. The Indian Junior Rodeo Association offers rodeos throughout the season for four age levels of competitors.

Young people gather on the sidelines.

The Big Foot Ride

One of the most powerful newer horse traditions is the Big Foot Memorial Ride—a tribute to Lakota ancestors killed during the Wounded Knee Massacre on December 29, 1890. During this modern, two-week December trek, dozens of riders follow the path taken by Lakota Chief Big Foot and his band, who traveled 287 miles from the Standing Rock Reservation to the Pine Ridge Reservation in South Dakota seeking safety after the death of the great chief Sitting Bull. Instead of receiving protection, chief Big Foot and his people were massacred.

The Big Foot ride began in 1986, inspired by the determination of several men from various tribes to honor those who died at Wounded Knee almost a hundred years earlier. Riders start on December 14 at the gravesite of Sitting Bull. They travel about twenty-five miles each day on horseback and are joined by other riders along the way, arriving at the Wounded Knee Memorial site on December 29, no matter how brutal the weather. In 2008, for example, the wind-chill temperature on the first three days reached fifty degrees below zero Fahrenheit—hard on horses as well as riders. That year one woman in her twenties said that if she could finish the ride, her upcoming law studies at Georgetown University would be easy by comparison. Rider Donaven Yellow spoke about his experience in 2007 at age fifteen: "A couple of times I didn't feel my toes. And my legs were shaking. I had a Gatorade in my pocket. I tried to take a drink, but it was frozen solid

The Big Foot Memorial Ride crosses over the Big Foot Pass into the Badlands.

Stirring up snow on the Big Foot Ride.

after a couple of hours. I was really thirsty that day, and I wasn't warm enough to keep it thawed out."

The adults who began the Big Foot Ride pledged to honor their ancestors by carrying out the grueling ride four times. The young riders who accompanied them want to keep up the tradition.

They see it as a daring venture that shows their ability to endure nature's hardships and to challenge themselves. Now, every year, young Indian people prove their endurance by following Big Foot's trail. As Ron His Horse Is Thunder, chairman of the Standing Rock Sioux Tribe, put it, "For many youth, it has become a rite of passage. . . . It teaches them fortitude, to go forward without complaining. It's so much a part of

Despite the cold, the participants enjoy the challenge.

TOP: Riders check out the trail on a frigid winter day during the Big Foot Ride.

BOTTOM: Time to saddle up for another cold day on the trail.

This image from David Dragonfly, *Stealing the Enemy's Horses,* evokes the history of the Blackfeet people.

who we are." With their horses, these young people are pursuing a path of pride in their cultural traditions.

As they continue their efforts to keep their cultures vibrant and meaningful in today's world, the Plains tribes will always be sure to include their most important animal partner — the horse — in their plans and in their dreams.

Books for Further Reading

Ancona, George. *Powwow.* New York: Harcourt Paperbacks, 1993.

Cooper, Michael L. *Indian School: Teaching the White Man's Way.* New York:
  Clarion Books, 1999.

Hungry Wolf, Beverly. *Daughters of the Buffalo Women: Maintaining the Tribal Faith.*
  Summertown, Tenn.: Book Publishing Company, 1997.

National Museum of the American Indian. *Do All Indians Live in Tipis?: Questions
  and Answers from the National Museum of the American Indian.* Washington, D.C.:
  National Museum of the American Indian, 2007.

Patent, Dorothy Hinshaw. *The Buffalo and the Indians: A Shared Destiny.* New York:
  Clarion Books, 2006.

Philip, Neil. *The Great Circle: A History of the First Nations.* New York:
  Clarion Books, 2006.

Reich, Susanna. *Painting the Wild Frontier: The Art and Adventures of George Catlin.*
  New York: Clarion Books, 2008.

Standing Bear, Luther. *My Indian Boyhood,* New Edition. Lincoln, Nebraska:
  Bison Books, 2006.

Terry, Michael. *Daily Life in a Plains Indian Village, 1868.* New York:
  Clarion Books, 1999.

Tohe, Laura. *No Parole Today.* New York: West End Press, 1999.

Waheenee. *Waheenee: An Indian Girl's Story (1921).* Whitefish, Montana:
  Kessinger Publishing, 2009.

Index

Page numbers in *italics* refer to photos and illustrations.